When the river spoke, I listened

Raquel Costa

BookLeaf Publishing

Presentation by *BookLeaf Publishing*

Web: www.bookleafpub.com

E-mail: info@bookleafpub.com

ISBN : 9789357445580

First edition 2022

DEDICATION

To all my students and teachers, thank you for growing with me.

I want to thank my family and my boyfriend Fernando above all for supporting me through all the changes and difficult moments of my life. I also want to thank my friends, now spread throughout the world. Your kindness made it possible to not only survive but also to thrive and grow. Being alone in a new place can be terrifying at times but thanks to you, I have been able to make a home, many homes, all over the world.
To my students, who have touched my heart deeply and without whom I would definitely not be here. I remember you all every single day and know that you are in my heart and in my prayers, always.
Lastly, to Bookleaf Publishing for making this book a reality. I couldn't have done it without you and I'm eternally grateful.

The bear

A bear in the forest never feels as alone as when he looks around
at the immense vastness of trees
It is his home but he never feels like he owns it, can never quite grasp it between his claws
Like a jumping fish
swooshing, sliding, slippering
He feels alone, he feels tiny, faced with the reverence of such immense mysteries

An endless landscape of adventures he can't even begin to imagine
But he doesn't fret, he doesn't fuss
He knows his place and it is right here, among the trees
His home is IN the unknown
And he likes it that way

The bear knows he is not alone
In fact bears, despite their big build and ferocious independence
are creatures of community
They wander, they may even be lost but they are never truly alone
That keeps him strong

No matter where he goes his family is close by
The unknown is their home too
whether they know it or not

We all belong in the wild, deep down
It is our heart that needs a place to root

Last day of summer

It always feels impossible when it arrives
like it contains a whole lifetime in it
like you've grown a whole year in a shapeless other dimension
And have to zap back to reality
You're never quite sure what this reality looks like
because it never looks like what you left behind
It's something entirely new
something you don't yet know how to put a name to

You feel, sometimes, like you've become a whole new person
Lost between the thin lines of every aspect of your being
A part of you wishes you could bathe under the summer sun forever
That you could be the smiley girl with the ankle bracelets and the tan
letting your long hair sway in the breeze,
brushing your back against your flowy flowery dress
As you dance these lukewarm nights away

As if they never existed, will never exist again
because they won't.

Another part of you wishes to be that woman
with her fresh new books and novelty pens
with a perfect first day outfit,
a fresh new planner and an ocean of possibility
It can sometimes be hard
to let the two oceans merge
and the two girls be friends
They promise they will write, or e-mail or call
but they always end up forgetting.

It's not their fault. Life gets in the way.
The world always makes you feel like
you have to choose
There is no such thing as a happy flowy girl at
work and no space for purpose on the beach
The world is wrong, you know this
and yet part of you always cries for your flowy
summer friend
I'll miss you so much, my dear
See you next year

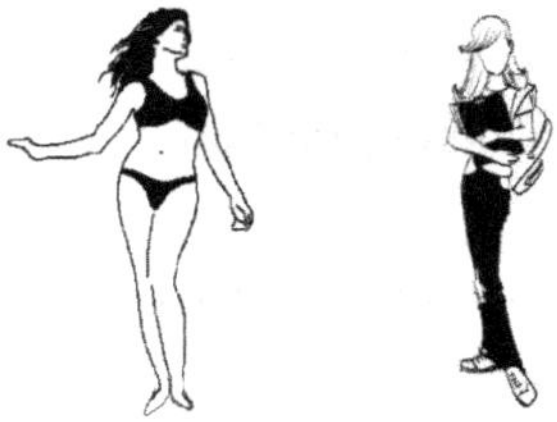

Alice in Wonderland

I can feel myself growing inside of my body
like a tree
My roots are spreading and I've never felt so
FREE
So alive, so full of life
All my life I looked for room to grow, expand
and
Here I am
my soul taking up so much room I hardly fit my
body anymore
Like Alice and that mushroom
I cannot stop growing towards the sky
Who knows where I'll go? Who knows
where the edges of my being really are?
(If there are any edges)
Today I feel I am limitless
My heart is rooted in the earth
but my hair is already green with
the leaves of trees
growing lighter and lighter towards the sky
I'm getting dizzy in the best way
My stomach is tight but I keep growing
up and up and up
and from this altitude

further from my little body than I've ever been
before
I finally see myself clearly

Fate

I remember this smell of damp grass and
the warmth of the setting sun
from when we sat, a year ago, carelessly lying
together and taking in this view

We didn't know I was fated to return so soon but
something started that day
Then and there the record started spinning and
the wheels began to turn
When I met you, Madrid, I didn't know we were
fated
I could feel the pull
There was a hint of destiny in our meeting
When we walked next to the Palace
And kissed at sunset
My lips dipped in gin
I said I could live here
I didn't mean the palace
Little did I know my wish would come true
In a year's time,
Here I am

Twenty pennies

Twenty pennies for a prayer
that this week will better than last one
Twenty pennies for a prayer for good health,
a steady breath and strong heart
steady legs to travel far and
powerful shoulders to carry the weight
of the day's challenges
Twenty pennies for my courage isn't enough
Twenty pennies for my love will never reach
But twenty pennies are not even needed
Just my feeble knees on the wooden rest
God is listening

20
EURO
CENT

No storm

I adore this autumn weather
Nothing smells quite as good
as the rain in September
And this moody sky
no longer joyous and blue but bright white
as if we lived inside a cloud
A world of our own
I miss being in my own little world
with you
in bed all day while it rained or snowed outside
The storm has nothing on us
It's impossible to feel cold when the heart is
warm
when your soul has cosy sheets to crawl into
and warm hands caressing your face
No storm can enter here

Clack, clack

Fresh books and coffee,
sharp suit, buttons done
sew shiny latest model sunglasses and bag
My shoes go
Clack, clack on the marble floor

It's a brand new dawn, it's a new day, it's a new
life and I'm feeling
TERRIFIED
I am a monster in high heels, an imposter with a
lipstick smile
A faker with perfect bag and perfect notebook,
perfect pens but my shoes go
Clack, clack on the marble floor

And all I hear is the hollow sound of knocking
on my bedroom door at night,
the sinister sound of someone finding out there
is not as much beyond
that door as expected
That the empress has no clothes, so to speak
Wait, what am I wearing?
When they knock on my door at night how will
they know who I am
or what I can do, dressed like this?

Is it too much or too little?
Am I right or am I wrong?
Am I colour or black or white?
Am I patterned or am I plain?

Clack, clack go my shoes
I'm getting closer
They will open the door, they will force it
I can already see the handle slowly painfully turning
like a knife digging into my side
What is beyond that door? What do they see?
Is it dust or is it me or just a version of me I've invented
To hide all the baggage I have to carry
Not the bags that bruised my legs or the ones that hang from my eyes
but those in my soul
as I leave the past behind

The sky is pretty colours

The sky is pretty colours tonight
and all I can think is I'd love to shout to you
Look at that orange
Look at that purple
Look at that blue
Aren't they amazing?
I would turn your face and stroke your beard and
kiss you gently
You would tell me "not as beautiful as you"
I would wrinkle my nose and cringe
but just a little

The sky is ours
It doesn't really matter what colour yours is
as opposed to mine
They are the same
I am with you singing my soul out
at that festival, my legs rested on your shoulders
and my hair flying in the evening air
And you are on this park bench,
sharing this melting paint pot of a sky
The sky is ours because we are together
The colours are ours and nothing else matters

The Flautist

I can see how that man that came to Hamelin
lured all the rats from the sewers
to a distant land
Just like the gentle soldier from the park
lures my worries and anxieties to
another dimension

I feel sleepy as if trapped in a spell
How can a stranger have such an effect
on my heart and body
I sway
The sounds of the flute give
the merest possibility
A hope that everything I've seen so far isn't all

I have always said
there is beauty and wonder to come but
to the sound of his flute
I can almost believe it

Why we don't fall

I hold onto little things
like raindrops and the coming autumn weather
like the regularity of buses and the common
courtesies of everyday life
A soft smile, a handshake and a good morning

When life feels overwhelming at least
it makes sense that the seasons change
or that the bus arrives on time
or that my morning tea tastes just the same
as it does on any other day
The irony is, everything still changes all the time
Even these daily regularities are irregularities
when analysed
Not twins, just siblings

Like a tightrope walker, the thing that keeps us
up is not stable at all
but we trust it nevertheless and trust ourselves
more
That's why we don't fall

Where am I?

These days I can't find myself
Not even on Google Maps or satellite
Not even with a GPS or Find my friend
I don't yet know where I am
There are traces of me spread through
every place I've ever been
Every city or town I've called home for even a
little while
There are bits of me
in every hug and kiss I ever felt
There are shards of my heart
in every goodbye I had to utter
with a shaky breath
And in every tear I shed,
wandering alone next to the Louvre
That day Blowing in the Wind was playing
and I could feel my heart ache for a friend I
feared I'd never see again
and for all the friends who walked with me
along the city of light
I'll never forget

I'm lost

There are better things ahead
There are beautiful, wonderful, dreams and
holidays and nights drinking with friends
There is beauty, there is wonder, there is fun
There is so much in the future, so much beauty,
so much…
Everything will be fine
is what
I repeat to myself everyday
But it's never quite enough to make up for the
hole in my heart and for the feeling
that
I'm lost
I'm lost I'm lost I'm lost

Restless

My head buzzing with fervent crazy breathless energy
I feel stuck and desperate
like I've been stuck in an invisible cage, the bars too strong to break through
I need to move, to dance, to run, to expand and to zap everywhere
Superspeed is my superpower except I don't know where to run

I want to be everywhere all at once but if you asked me where I couldn't pinpoint a single place
I could not even begin to list my interminable roll of ideas and fantasies of what I'd like to do
Everything is perfect and terrible at once in these moments
It feels like ecstasy mixed in with a desperate desire to make it all better, make it all perfect
Today, immediately, right NOW

When my demons come knocking this energy turns dark and stabs me,
five times in the gut with no chance to
stop the flow

That I’m not worthy, that I’ll never do it, that
I’m not enough, nobody likes me and
what is there to like anyway?
How can I be better, be enough, be perfect today,
immediately and right NOW

The trick this time is not
to bring the future to me but to erase it
completely
The now can stop my head spinning
At 100 miles an hour and pick a speed
more appropriate for residential roads
It takes me a while to drive back and I know
I’ll feel the need to go out again sometime soon
To purge this energy that invades my body and
explodes like fireworks
For now, however, I’ll try to stay closer to home

We get acquainted

I take a breath into my heart
just in case I can feel something, anything over
all this noise
Around me there is a sea of new faces and they
talk, oh they talk and talk and talk

I read lately that we are reflections of what
others think we are
but all I see everyday are strange faces
and a reflection of me I've never met
I don't quite know what to say to this person
or how to approach her
I guess I've always been a little shy
with strangers
Or have I?

This girl I've never met seems shameless and
confident
She knows what she's doing, she knows what to
say
Her voice is rugged and loud and clear like I've
never heard it before
and yet I can't recognise myself in her
She is able to verbalise to perfection everything
I've ever wanted to say

She doesn’t choke or quiver or trip over steps or
crash into doors
She never woke up with unexplainable bruises
the next day
I’m sure in fact that there is nothing this girl
couldn’t explain

She loves to talk, just like me,
little chatterboxes both of us
But unlike me her words don’t get muddled up
in her mouth
spinning round and round like clothes in a
washing machine
They come out clear and sharp like lightning
They hit the spot just right without taking
side trips
Her words are the sharp clear pictures on an
Iphone I’ve never owned
While mine are a blurry Polaroid picture

Sometimes I want to be like her
Other days I don’t want her anywhere near me
I’ve been avoiding her lately
but I think it's time
we start to get acquainted

Solo saxophone

They played our song on a solo saxophone
just like in Miss. Saigon
When I heard it the first time I cried
The couples caressing on park benches see
through
the rose-coloured glasses I left in Paris
along with my old printer
and the smile I left on the streets on England

The open voice of the instrument reminds me of
your head thrown back when you laugh
like a child without a care in the world
You don't care who watches and
now I watch the people,
carelessly throwing their heads back
with laughter

I will bring this memory back many times
When my own lips and hands caress the sides of
a sax
and bring out the sounds of Madrid
Just like that sax
etched into my heart, wherever I am in the world

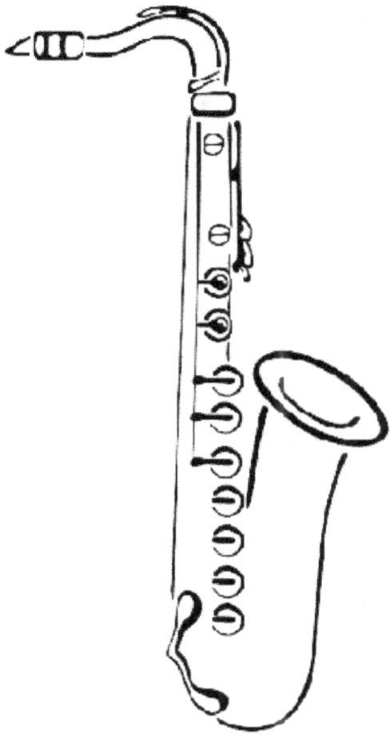

Pre-sunset

Sweet notes float through the air on this warm
Sunday afternoon
I hear the bells toll from the palace
and shouts in the distance
The contrast is so intense and yet so
overwhelmingly beautiful
I wish to ask that flautist
how he rode his bike to this spot on such a
gorgeous afternoon
just to play me such a light, fluffy tune
The sounds of Madrid are so diverse but
so raw and honest
both hard and soft
gentle and majestic

The chants of football songs sung by a students
holding flags
coexist with the giggles at a kid's birthday party

In these moments I think there is so much
harmony in opposites
The instruments playing at the same time create
an orchestra of sound
that makes up us, all of us

A part of something larger
or perhaps we just are
Larger than life

Connected through this music, the warm breeze
and the sounds of the city
The sun is ready to set in a few hours and close
yet another lifetime of a week

Home

She sang I saw the signs
and it opened up my eyes to
how unbelievable it is
that a simple smile or a hug can create a home
that once was empty
Love and light fills every corner
when kind hearts unite
and friends become family
Careless laughs and nights watching movies
with butter popcorn
I thought my brothers were far away and I
never had a sister
but back home is becoming here at home
More and more I don't have far to travel
Home is here

Let go

My limbs stretch every morning as a way
to find meaning so my soul stays
So it finds a safe place
to cry and break apart and discover
the meaning of
why I am here
Immersed in my fear but fighting and learning
and growing
They say I am a warrior
so I adjust my stance
My fight is my fight is my fight
It looks easy for some and impossible for others
For me it's a journey
to let go of heavy anchors that keep me tied
and in lightness find definition
and understanding

The more baggage we carry the harder it is
to see anything clearly
All we see is swirls of colour and sound and
words, too many
I want a simple phrase
to carry me through today
because tomorrow will take care of itself
Let go

Savage sky

What a savage sky
How should I be so lucky as to be
invited here
as if it were so simple
1 plus 1 is 2
The river summons you
and the sky puts on a show
as it always does
dressing itself
in the bright white dress of early autumn
and a moody scarf of grey clouds
How can this great sky make an appearance
so easily
looking gorgeous
leaving me breathless and speechless
when some days I struggle to even get out of bed

I know
I have not honoured this place as I should
Its savage sacredness mocks me
As if I could put pen to paper
at will
and make sense of this chaos called life
The sky laughs and the river smirks
They know

I surrender
willingly
because
deep
down
I know
I belong
Here

The river ate my poem

The river ate my poem
I wanted to dedicate it
To the Manzanares
Flowing shallow but steady close to my house
But the river had other plans
At this time of day
I swear I hear God in the silence
The peace of the river speaks to me in ways I
cannot explain
It tells me to watch and listen
The river never lied when it showed me
to come here
So I return as if by magic to the bridge
bathing my past and future in sunsets and the
full moon

Bridging the gap
between who I was and who I might be

Because I wouldn't shut up,
the river ate my poem
and chided me sternly but gently
Sunsets are to be watched and felt, not written

An open letter

Dear Porto,
I wish I got to know you
the way you've always known me from the day
I blinked slowly for the first time
When I broke, you glued the corners of my
paper heart back together
So I could try again at love

Dear Alverca,
I'll always be an innocent in your eyes.
No matter where I go my heart will always have
a home
in that pink bedroom with a coat rack
that looked like a man in a hat
My childhood stories splayed across the bed
My head reeling as I fell in love for the first time
with the smell of ink on yellowed pages
and the sound of trains through the night
I always imagined where they were travelling
I never imagined I'd be travelling myself

Dear Cardiff,
I will remember you am byth
From a fragile Do Not Touch moving box you
created a small home,

a chance of something special
I won't say I didn't want to run
at first
and live a different life
But you showed me a possibility of being happy
that there are always smiles willing to build you
a home
Brick by brick, key by key
the notes floated on my piano to the sound of a
thousand nights
thinking about a boy on my bedroom window
As the rain tapped lightly on the glass
To Taylor Swift and sleepovers
and my first poems
They sounded nothing like this

Dear Tonbridge,
You taught me I'm a fighter, above all
that no matter what demons haunt me or what I
think of myself
I can always come out victorious
but knowing that not every victory is
worth the fight
That was a lesson I had to bleed for

Dear Southampton,
You won me over with the smell of the sea
and the first kiss that made my head spin

Friendships over pints showed me how
I could be myself again

Dear Paris,
I'll never forget how I felt inside Orsay
or how the lights sparkled on the river every
metro journey and Monday night
Christmas markets and plastic trees
My heart flew back to all the corners of the
world

Dear Madrid,
When the river spoke, I listened
and I'll keep listening as long as you'll have me
Or forever, whichever comes first.

www.ingramcontent.com/pod-product-compliance
Lightning Source LLC
Chambersburg PA
CBHW051739130826
49812CB00033B/919
9789357445580